Drip, Drip, Drop
EARTH'S WATER

The Water Beneath Your Feet

by Ellen Lawrence

Consultant:

Shawn W. Wallace
Department of Earth and Planetary Sciences
American Museum of Natural History
New York, New York

BEARPORT
PUBLISHING

New York, New York

Credits

Cover, © kavram/Shutterstock; 4, © Algefoto/Shutterstock; 5, © Artens/Shutterstock; 6, © Nattapol Sritongcom/Shutterstock; 7, © Filipe B. Varela/Shutterstock, © Ralf Maassen (DTEurope)/Shutterstock, © Whyjeep/Shutterstock, and © Masson/Shutterstock; 8, © Patryk Kosmider/Shutterstock; 9, © Masson/Shutterstock, © Angelo Sarnacchiaro/Shutterstock, and © Sararwut Jaimassiri/Shutterstock; 10T, © Masson/Shutterstock, © Angelo Sarnacchiaro/Shutterstock, and © Sararwut Jaimassiri/Shutterstock; 10B, © Paul Prescott/Shutterstock; 11, © tr3gin/Shutterstock; 12, © kavram/Shutterstock; 13, © fllphoto/Shutterstock; 14, © Gilles Paire/Shutterstock; 15, © Ariadne Van Zandbergen/FLPA; 16, © Khalil Mazraawi/Getty Images; 17, © Rudy Umans/Shutterstock; 18T, © Gavin Baker Photography/Shutterstock; 18B, © Nielskliim/Shutterstock; 19, © kanvag/Shutterstock; 20, © nortongo/Shutterstock; 21, © LOOK Die Bildagentur der Fotografen GmbH/Alamy; 22, © Ruby Tuesday Books; 23TL, © Masson/Shutterstock, © Angelo Sarnacchiaro/Shutterstock, and © Sararwut Jaimassiri/Shutterstock; 23TC, © Christopher Ewing/Shutterstock; 23TR, © Matthew Cole/Shutterstock; 23BL, © africa294/Shutterstock; 23BC, © Belovodchenko Anton/Shutterstock; 23BR, © Alexander Raths/Shutterstock.

Publisher: Kenn Goin
Editor: Jessica Rudolph
Creative Director: Spencer Brinker
Design: Emma Randall
Photo Researcher: Ruby Tuesday Books Ltd

Library of Congress Cataloging-in-Publication Data

Names: Lawrence, Ellen, 1967– author.
Title: The water beneath your feet / by Ellen Lawrence.
Description: New York, New York : Bearport Publishing, [2016] | Series: Drip, drip, drop: Earth's water | Audience: Ages 6–10. | Includes bibliographical references and index.
Identifiers: LCCN 2015040334 (print) | LCCN 2015041638 (ebook) | ISBN 9781943553242 (library binding) | ISBN 9781943553587 (ebook)
Subjects: LCSH: Groundwater—Juvenile literature. | Aquifers—Juvenile literature. | Hydrologic cycle—Juvenile literature. | Water—Juvenile literature.
Classification: LCC GB1003.8 .L39 2016 (print) | LCC GB1003.8 (ebook) | DDC 551.48—dc23
LC record available at http://lccn.loc.gov/2015040334

For more information, write to Bearport Publishing Company, Inc., 45 West 21st Street, Suite 3B, New York, New York 10010. Printed in the United States of America.

10 9 8 7 6 5 4 3 2 1

Contents

From Sky to Ground

When it rains, water falls from the sky and splashes onto the ground.

The rainwater soaks into flowerbeds.

It trickles down cracks in sidewalks and roads.

You can't see the water, but it's still there—underground!

This water, called groundwater, is very important to life on Earth.

There are two main types of water on Earth. Salt water contains lots of salt. It is found in oceans and saltwater lakes. Fresh water is found in ponds, rivers, and some lakes. Most groundwater is fresh water.

freshwater lake

Trickling Down and Down

Under the ground, rainwater trickles between tiny spaces in the **soil**.

The water moves down and down to the rocky layers beneath the soil.

It trickles between gravel and stones, and seeps into tiny cracks in rocks.

Eventually, the groundwater reaches solid rock and can go no farther.

Without groundwater, plants could not survive. Trees, grass, and other plants take in water from the soil with their roots.

rain

roots

water trickling
through soil

water seeping into
cracks in rock

gravel and stones

solid rock

Besides trickling into the soil when it rains, in what
other ways do you think water can get into the ground?
(You will find some ideas on page 24.)

On the Move

Once water is in the ground, it doesn't always stay in one place.

Groundwater may collect hundreds of feet below the surface.

It might seep between gravel and rocks, moving sideways until it reaches a pond or lake.

The water may trickle into a stream or river and even end up in an ocean.

ocean

How Water Moves Underground

lake

soil

ocean

gravel and rocks

Groundwater that collects deep below Earth's surface might stay underground for thousands or even millions of years!

water collecting deep underground

solid rock

Aquifers and Springs

A large amount of underground water that collects in one place is called an **aquifer**.

Water in aquifers collects in spaces between gravel and rocks.

In some places, aquifer water escapes to the surface.

This water—called a spring—can form a tiny pond or a large lake.

aquifer

spring

pond

solid rock

spring

Sometimes, a spring bubbles to the surface in a hot, dry desert. Then plants are able to grow around the water, forming a place called an oasis.

Geysers

Sometimes, water from a spring spurts high into the air. Why?

Deep underground, beneath Earth's layer of solid rock, there is super-hot liquid rock called **magma**.

In some places, magma rises into cracks in the rock and gets close to the surface.

Then the magma heats the water in a spring until it boils and spurts up.

This fountain of boiling water is called a geyser.

geyser

1. Steam rises from a pool of boiling-hot spring water.
2. The boiling water starts to bubble up.
3. Water bursts into the air.

At Yellowstone Park in Wyoming, there is a famous geyser called Old Faithful. About every 90 minutes, it shoots scorching-hot water up to 185 feet (56 m) in the air!

The water used in many homes and businesses is taken from the ground. Yet, the water doesn't come from a spring or geyser. How do you think people get water from deep underground?

Old Faithful

Building a Well

People can bring groundwater to the surface by building a well.

To do this, workers dig a deep, narrow hole down into an aquifer.

Then a long pipe is put down the hole into the water.

Finally, a **pump** on the surface draws the water up the pipe—like sucking water up a straw.

pipe

workers building a well

handle

pump

water

In some places, people get water from a well by moving the pump's handle up and down. Water gushes from the pump and can then be collected.

Getting Water

Many people in the United States get their water in a different way.

At a place called a water treatment plant, large machines pump groundwater to the surface.

Then the water is cleaned so that it's free of dirt and germs.

Finally, the water is carried through pipes to homes and farms.

People use this water for drinking and washing and for watering crops.

These huge machines are pumping underground water.

Farms and cities use lots of underground water. Fortunately, aquifers get refilled when it rains. In some places, however, people are using groundwater faster than the aquifers can fill up. This can cause water shortages.

This machine is spraying water on farm crops.

water

Sometimes groundwater can become unsafe for people to use. How do think this might happen?

Water in Danger

Sometimes, groundwater can become so badly **polluted** that people cannot use it.

How does this happen?

Many farmers spray chemicals on their fields to kill pests.

These chemicals soak into the soil and mix with groundwater.

Also, tanks and pipes filled with **sewage** can leak and pollute groundwater.

a plane spraying chemicals on crops

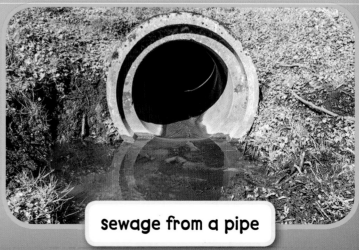

sewage from a pipe

Often, garbage from homes and businesses is taken to landfills. When rainwater trickles through the trash, the groundwater below the landfill can become polluted.

garbage at a landfill

Precious Groundwater

People, animals, and plants all need fresh water to survive.

Almost one third of the fresh water on Earth is groundwater.

Therefore, it's very important that we use it wisely.

Next time you see rainwater soaking into the ground, remember that it hasn't disappeared.

That water might one day become the water you drink!

The largest aquifer in the world is in Australia. It's called the Great Artesian Basin and it's almost the size of Alaska! This aquifer is an important source of water for people who live in dry desert areas.

Australia

The blue area shows the size of the Great Artesian Basin.

This spring in Australia bubbles up from the Great Artesian Basin.

Science Lab

You can see how groundwater collects in an aquifer by making a model.

Make Your Own Aquifer

1. Ask an adult to cut off the top part of a 2-liter (4 pt) bottle and tape over the sharp edge with duct tape. Then ask the adult to cut out five pea-sized holes in the bottle about I inch (2.5 cm) from the bottom.

2. Put about 4 inches (10 cm) of gravel mixed with sand in the bottom of the bottle. The mixture should be about two-thirds gravel and one-third sand.

3. Next, add a 4-inch (10 cm) layer of potting soil.

4. Stand the bottle in a bowl.

5. Slowly trickle 1/2 cup (118 ml) of water, colored with food coloring, over the soil, and observe what happens.

You will need:

- An empty 2-liter (4 pt) plastic bottle
- Scissors and an adult helper
- Duct tape
- A small spade
- Gravel, sand, and potting soil
- A bowl
- A jug filled with 1/2 cup (118 ml) of water, with five drops of blue food coloring added
- A notebook and pencil

What do you think will happen to the water?

Write your predictions in your notebook. Leave your model overnight and check it the next day.

What do you observe in the bottle? Did what happened match your predictions?

Has any of the water trickled out of the holes?

How is your model like an aquifer?

(The answers to the questions are on page 24.)

plastic bottle

soil

sand and gravel

holes

Science Words

aquifer (A-kwuh-fur) an underground area where large amounts of groundwater collect

magma (MAG-muh) super-hot liquid rock located deep inside Earth

polluted (puh-LOOT-id) made dirty by chemicals, oil, sewage, or garbage

pump (PUMP) a mechanical device used to suck water up from underground

sewage (SOO-idj) liquid and solid human waste that is flushed down toilets and carried away in pipes

soil (SOYL) the top layer of Earth's surface in which plants grow; soil is mostly made of tiny bits of rock

Index

Read More

Levete, Sarah. *A Tale of One Well in Malawi (The Big Picture)*. Mankato, MN: Capstone (2010).

Nadeau, Isaac. *Water Under Ground (The Water Cycle)*. New York: PowerKids Press (2003).

Nelson, Robin. *Water (First Step Nonfiction: What Earth Is Made Of)*. Minneapolis, MN: Lerner (2005).

Learn More Online

To learn more about water under the ground, visit
www.bearportpublishing.com/DripDripDrop

About the Author

Ellen Lawrence lives in the United Kingdom. Her favorite books to write are those about animals and nature. In fact, the first book Ellen bought for herself, when she was six years old, was the story of a gorilla named Patty Cake that was born in New York's Central Park Zoo.

Answers

Page 7: When ice or snow melts, this water trickles into the ground. When you use a sprinkler or hose to water garden plants, this water also soaks into the ground.

Page 22: Just like rain, the water trickled through the soil. Then it collected in the sand and gravel. You may not be able to see all of the water—but it's there. Just like in an aquifer under the ground, the water collects between the stones and grains of sand. Some of the water may even trickle out of the holes. Groundwater travels far underground, too, and may eventually end up in rivers, lakes, and oceans.